The Boat Book

Samantha Berger • Pamela Chanko

Scholastic Inc.
New York • Toronto • London • Auckland • Sydney

Acknowledgments

Literacy Specialist: Linda Cornwell

National Science Consultant: David Larwa

Design: Silver Editions

Photo Research: Amla Sanghvi

Endnotes: Paul Hack

Endnote Illustrations: Craig Spearing

Photographs: **Cover:** Suzanne & Nick Geary/Tony Stone Images; p. 1: Harald Sund/Image Bank; p. 2: Don Hebert/FPG International; p. 3: Kevin Miller/Tony Stone Images; p. 4: Gunnar Keith/FPG International; p. 5: Jeri Gleiter/FPG International; p. 6: Oli Tennent/Tony Stone Images/Sunseeker Powerboats; p. 7: Suzanne & Nick Geary/Tony Stone Images; p. 8: Ariel Skelley/The Stock Market; p. 9: Per Eriksson/Image Bank; p. 10: Ken Straiton/The Stock Market; p. 11: Harvey Lloyd/The Stock Market; p. 12: Will & Deni McIntyre/Tony Stone Images.

Library of Congress Cataloging-in-Publication Data
Berger, Samantha.
The boat book/Samantha Berger, Pamela Chanko.
p.cm. --(Science emergent readers)
Summary: Simple text and photographs introduce different kinds of
boats and how they are propelled through the water by sails, oars, motors, etc.
ISBN 0-439-08125-4 (pbk.: alk. paper)
1. Boats and boating--Juvenile literature. 2. Ships--Juvenile literature. 3. Ship propulsion--Juvenile literature. [1. Boats and boating. 2. Ships.] I. Chanko, Pamela, 1968-. II. Title. III. Series.
VM150.B48 1999
623.8--dc21
98-53312
CIP AC

4   5   6   7   8   9   10   08   03   02   01   00   99

What do boats need to move?

This boat needs sails to move.

This boat does, too.

This boat needs paddles to move.

This boat does, too.

This boat needs a motor to move.

This boat does, too.

This boat needs oars to move.

This boat does, too.

This boat needs steam to move.

This boat does, too.

What does this boat need to move?

The Boat Book

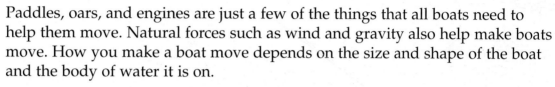

Paddles, oars, and engines are just a few of the things that all boats need to help them move. Natural forces such as wind and gravity also help make boats move. How you make a boat move depends on the size and shape of the boat and the body of water it is on.

Riverboats Riverboats, also called paddle wheelers, are large, often flat-bottomed boats, most likely to be found on long stretches of wide rivers. Although river currents can move them slowly downstream, greater speeds and upstream movement are attained by the use of a paddle wheel. As the engine-driven wheel turns, the paddles push against the water, causing the boat to move forward.

Sailboats Sailboats use the powerful force of wind to move them along the water. Sails are made of large pieces of fabric that are designed to catch the wind. When the wind fills the sails, it pushes them—and the boat—forward. The shape of the sail allows sailboats to change direction and also to stay on a steady course if the wind direction changes.

Paddles Paddles are used to make boats such as canoes and kayaks move. The paddles push back on the water and make the boat move forward. Paddling on one side of the boat will make the boat turn in the opposite direction. If you keep paddling on just one side, the boat will turn in a circle. To go forward, you must alternate paddle strokes from one side of the boat to the other. River rafters use paddles to help them steer as the swift current carries them quickly downstream.

Motors Motors make boats move at great speeds. The motor turns a propeller that is below the surface of the water at the rear of the boat. As the propeller turns at high speed, it pushes the water away, and the boat moves forward. The fastest motorboats, or speedboats, have been known to go more than 300 miles per hour!

Oars Oars are similar to paddles, but they are larger and are used to move heavier boats. Making the boat move by pulling the oar through the water is called rowing. Some rowboats have only two oars and are small enough for one person to row. Larger rowboats have many oars and require a team of rowers. Teams of rowers all row their oars at the same time, greatly increasing the boat's speed. During races, a person at the front of the boat, called a coxswain, makes sure that all the team members row together.

Steam The first boats to use engines were steamboats. When water is heated to 100 degrees Celsius, it is transformed into a gas called steam. If water is heated in a closed container, the steam expands and takes up more space than the water it came from. This causes excess pressure to build up inside the container. A jet of steam can then be released through a valve and used to spin turbines, which are like big propellers. The turbines are connected to shafts that turn smaller propellers on the outside of the boat. When a propeller spins, it pushes the water away, causing the boat to move forward.

Tugboats Sometimes boats rely on other boats to help them move. When large boats enter or leave harbors, they are not able to navigate the narrow channels. A boat that pushes or pulls another boat is called a tugboat. Often two tugboats will team up to help maneuver a larger boat. Typically, one tug pushes the ship from the back, and the other pulls it from the front. This ensures that the large ship travels a straight course. It is also the job of a tugboat to tow disabled ships that can no longer move on their own.